A Short Course
In Happiness

Practical Steps To
A Happier Life

Lynda Wallace

Some of the chapters in this book appeared previously in slightly different form in *Taste for Life* Magazine or on the website activehappiness.com. Reprinted with permission.

Books published by Three Sixty Five are available at special quantity discounts to use as premiums and sales promotions or for use in corporate training programs.

ISBN: 0988982315
ISBN-13: 978-0988982314

This book is printed on acid-free paper.

For Evie

ABOUT THE AUTHOR

Be yourself. Everyone else is already taken.

Oscar Wilde

Lynda Wallace is a Certified Positive Psychology Coach. She works with clients who are experiencing changes or pursuing goals in their personal or professional lives and want to make the next chapter of their lives the best yet. Lynda meets with clients both in-person and by phone or video.

Before her own career change, Lynda was a longtime executive with Johnson & Johnson, where she was responsible for a highly successful portfolio of global businesses including Band-Aids, Neosporin, and Purell. She holds an MBA from the Wharton School of the University of Pennsylvania.

Lynda is a very happy single mother; she and her daughter live in Montclair, NJ.

Please visit lyndawallace.com to get in touch with Lynda, read about her coaching practice, register for a workshop, or schedule a consultation. She would love to hear from you.

CONTENTS

INTRODUCTION
THE FOUR ELEMENTS OF HAPPINESS

You can't stop the waves,
but you can learn how to surf.

Jon Kabat-Zinn

The Practical Science of Happiness

What really makes people happy, and how can we create greater happiness in our lives and the lives of those we care about?

These questions are at the heart of the work being done by researchers in the field of Positive Psychology, who apply the rigorous methods of social science to the study of happiness and well-being. Their findings are practical, encouraging, and sometimes surprising. And they've led to the development of proven techniques we can all use to become more optimistic, reduce our anxiety, enhance our relationships, achieve goals that matter to us, and take other steps that can help us to transform how we experience our lives.

Our *Short Course in Happiness* will be a journey through some of the most important research findings and most useful techniques from across Positive Psychology and related fields.

My emphasis is on the practical truths of happiness. So I only share insights and recommend techniques that are proven to work, and that I've successfully applied in my own life as well as in my work with clients. I've seen and experienced the impact of taking these steps, which is why I'm so delighted to have the opportunity to share them in this book.

Let's begin with a quick look at some of the benefits of happiness. Then we'll spend the rest of the book focusing on how to cultivate it.

The Benefits of Happiness

Not only is happiness obviously worth having for its own sake, it's also a powerful contributor to many of the other things we seek in life.

Happy people have stronger relationships with their spouses and friends and raise happier, more productive kids. They're more effective leaders, make better decisions, set and achieve higher goals, and even earn more money.

Happy people are also more fit and energetic, and less likely to develop chronic diseases. They even donate more money to charity and spend more time volunteering for causes they care about.

And happiness isn't just a *result* of these good things; it's also an important *cause* of them. In other words, by learning to be happier – which research has convincingly shown we can successfully do – we can also improve our relationships, benefit our families, and become healthier and more successful.

The Four Elements of Happiness

One of the most effective ways to figure out how to create greater happiness in our lives is to ask what very happy people have in common. Luckily for us, the answers to this question are quite clear – clear enough, in fact, that we can describe four common characteristics. I call them the *Four Elements of Happiness*, and I'll address one of them in each of the four sections of this book.

Here are the four things very happy people do:

1. Focus on the Positive

2. Cope Effectively with the Negative

3. Develop Strong Relationships

4. Pursue Meaningful Goals

We'll start our investigation of these four elements by looking at some common myths about happiness.

Myth #1: Happiness Is About Getting the Big Things Right

It's natural to think that if we were suddenly rich, beautiful, and living on the beach somewhere, *then* we'd be happy. But as it turns out, that type of good fortune has a surprisingly small impact on happiness.

Unless we're in truly intolerable situations, we can have a much bigger impact on our happiness by cultivating positive emotional outlooks and habits than we can by changing the "big things," such as where we live, how we look, and how much we earn.

Section One will focus on proven steps we can take to cultivate the positive in our lives.

Myth #2: Happy People Suppress Negative Emotions

Happy people actually experience sadness, grief, worry, and other so-called negative emotions nearly as frequently as unhappy people do. The difference is what happens once those negative feelings kick in.

Happier people are generally able to experience negative feelings without losing their hope for the future. They give themselves permission to feel sad, angry, or lonely, but they remain confident that things will get better. As a result, their sadness progresses into hope and action rather than regressing into anxiety and despair.

We'll find out how they do it, and how we can, too, in Section Two.

Myth #3: Pursuing Happiness is Self-Centered

The clearest of all conclusions drawn by researchers into emotional well-being is that our happiness is determined more by our relationships with other people than by any other single factor. The happiest people have good, trusting relationships at the center of their lives.

Those relationships may be with friends, spouses, or other family members; it doesn't much matter. What *does* matter is that we have people we know we can rely on for love and understanding, and who rely on us in turn.

In Section Three, we'll see how to cultivate the strong relationships that can make life so good.

Myth #4: I'll be Happy When I Achieve My Goals

Have you ever worked hard to achieve a goal, sure that its achievement would make you happy forever – or at least for a very long time – then wondered why the happiness didn't last? Or have you ever failed to achieve a long-sought goal and felt as if you'd never recover from the disappointment, only to discover before too long that the failure didn't ruin your life after all?

Committed goal pursuit is one of the keys to a happy life. But most of the happiness we get from our goals comes while we're making progress toward them, not after we achieve them. So it's important that we choose goals that we'll enjoy pursuing, and that are in synch with our most important values and priorities.

Section Four will focus on how we can most effectively set, pursue, and achieve personally meaningful goals.

So let's get to it, shall we? It's time to begin our Short Course in Happiness.

SECTION ONE
CULTIVATE THE POSITIVE

You won't find happiness where you're going
unless you first cultivate it where you are.

Unknown

Attitude and Action

Our outlooks, including our thoughts and attitudes, have tremendous potential to change how happy we are. Appreciating the many good things in our lives, learning not to obsess about worries and hurt feelings, and generally expecting positive outcomes with the confidence that we'll be able to cope even if things don't turn out as we wish — all of these habits of mind are essential to living our happiest lives. And a healthy, positive outlook on life can lead us to take the concrete actions necessary to be even happier.

Genuine happiness isn't about convincing ourselves that everything is great and choosing to live with things just as they are. People who recognize issues, problems, and opportunities – and act on them – are much happier than people who ignore them. So along with having a positive outlook, we need to make positive choices and take positive actions in our day-to-day lives.

Certain actions and habits are almost guaranteed to make us happier people. Actively nurturing our relationships, making it a priority to spend time doing things we enjoy with people we love, engaging in meaningful work (whether as an employee, a parent, or a volunteer), getting regular exercise, making progress toward lifelong goals and ambitions — all of these actions have an enormous impact on our happiness and well-being. And every one of them is made easier, more enjoyable, and more achievable with a positive attitude. Positive thoughts and positive actions go hand in hand and build on each other in ways that can transform our lives.

In this section, we'll look at how we can all develop the strengths and resources that underlie positive attitudes and actions. First stop: Optimism.

1
OPTIMISM

The happiest people don't have the best of everything;
they make the best of everything.

Unknown

How Optimistic Are You?

Optimism is a powerfully beneficial approach to life. It's well established that optimistic people are happier, healthier, and more successful than pessimists. And optimism is much more than just looking on the bright side of things. It's an approach to life that focuses on solutions rather than problems and spurs us on to take action to create the lives we want to live.

Of course, we can all be optimistic or pessimistic, depending on the situation. But there are certain habits of mind common to people with generally optimistic attitudes.

Take this quiz to see what they are – and if you've got them.

Question #1: Setback at Work

Your boss is dissatisfied with a big presentation you worked really hard on. You agree that it didn't go very well.

Is your reaction more like A or B?

A. You worry that your boss has lost confidence in you because of the poor presentation, and you wonder if you should start looking for another job – preferably one that doesn't require you to make presentations.

B. You let your boss know you're disappointed in how it went, but that you're confident that you can do better. You develop a plan to enhance your presentation skills and offer to take on an extra project that would give you a chance to make another – better – presentation sometime soon.

When pessimists think about problems, they tend to see them as general *("My boss has lost confidence in me")* and permanent *("I'd better look for another job")*.

Optimists, on the other hand, generally see problems as specific *("That presentation didn't go well")* and temporary *("I need to get better at this and then demonstrate my improved skills")*.

Optimists also tend to see failures as learning opportunities, and to have the confidence and determination to take advantage of them to create a better future.

Question #2: Delay at the Airport

You arrive at the airport to start your vacation and discover that your flight is delayed by three hours because your plane had equipment trouble and the airline has decided to swap it out for a different one.

Is your response more like A or B?

- A. "It's just my luck – this sort of thing always happens to me."

- B. "It's a pain, but these things happen to everybody. And I'd rather be on the ground because of a malfunctioning plane than up in the air in one."

Pessimists tend to take bad luck personally, convinced that they're uniquely likely to wind up in the long line at the grocery store or with bad weather on vacation, as if the universe is somehow conspiring to ruin their plans.

Optimists, on the other hand, recognize that these frustrations are random and not worth making ourselves miserable over. And they can usually find something to be grateful for, even when everything isn't going their way.

Question #3: Thanksgiving Disaster?

You're cooking a fabulous Thanksgiving dinner for your extended family. It's early afternoon, and time to peel the potatoes, when you realize you forgot to buy any.

Are you more likely to:

    A. Feel defeated. What's Thanksgiving without mashed potatoes? And of course the stores are closed. All your hard work to create a perfect holiday has been wasted.

    B. Figure everyone on your block is making mashed potatoes today, and that if they can each spare one potato, you can round up all you need in about ten minutes of ringing doorbells. And if that doesn't work, there will be plenty of other great things to eat.

On an emotionally pitched day like Thanksgiving, a pessimist is likely to get stuck in the feelings of embarrassment and frustration that can come with a mistake like this, and have a hard time thinking of ways to change the situation.

An optimist is able to think beyond the problem to possible solutions, including considering how friends and neighbors might be able to help turn the situation around. And if the fix doesn't pan out, the optimist is able to keep the problem in perspective and not let it ruin a great day.

So did you catch them all? In the answers to these three questions, we saw ten things that optimistic people do. Here they are.

Optimistic people:

    1. See problems as specific rather than general.

2. Consider setbacks to be temporary instead of permanent.

3. See failures as learning opportunities.

4. Have confidence in their ability to create a better future.

5. Take specific and determined action to do so.

6. Understand that bad luck is random and affects us all.

7. Find reasons to be grateful even in frustrating situations.

8. Think beyond problems to potential solutions.

9. Rely on friends and neighbors for help.

10. Keep problems in perspective.

Optimism leads to greater confidence, more determined action, and an ability to think of more creative solutions to problems. And of course all of those things lead in turn to greater optimism.

It's a self-reinforcing cycle, and the more we practice the habits of optimism, the more optimistic – and the happier, healthier, and more successful – we'll become.

How to Do It

Okay, so we've seen what optimistic people do, but how can we learn to do those things ourselves? Here's a five-step process for practicing the art of optimism in the face of life's inevitable letdowns.

1. Get Some Perspective

When things go wrong, it's easy to feel like catastrophe has struck. So the first thing to do is to try to take the long view. Is this setback going to matter in week, a month, or a year? Is it really the ruin of everything, or is it just one of the inevitable challenges that come with living a full life?

Remind yourself of the many times you've proven how resilient you are, and that you'll bounce back from this, too.

2. Get Creative

Dream up an unexpected way that the situation you're in could lead to something wonderful. Is the friend who helped you get through your divorce moving out of state? Maybe when you go to visit her she'll introduce you to her new also-divorced neighbor, who'll turn out to be just the kind of person you've been hoping to meet.

It doesn't matter how far-fetched the story is. The point is to remind yourself that life is unpredictable, and that most of the best things in your life would never have happened if things had gone according to plan. You're going to miss your friend an awful lot, but life's full of unexpected twists and turns, and you have no idea what good might come of her move.

3. Get Specific

Think about what went wrong and why. Say you just made a failed pitch to a prospective client. If you're feeling pessimistic, your first response may be that you lost the pitch because you're incompetent. That thinking is self-defeating and a bit of an easy way out, because if the reason is as big as that, there's not an awful lot you can do about it.

So get more specific about what happened. Did you have all of the necessary information about the client's needs before you prepared the pitch? If not, was there some way you could have better understood what she was looking for before you developed your presentation? And if you understand her needs better now, is there a way to confidently get back in front of her with a great new proposal?

Getting specific about what happened and why can help you to find ways to turn the current situation around and put you in a position to do better next time.

4. Get Going

Now it's time to figure out where you want to go from here. Are there insights you can gain from the setback that you can use to make your life even better than it would have been if things had gone as you'd hoped? Does the experience offer greater clarity about how to better achieve your goals, or even a new way to think about what's most important to you?

And finally, given the reality of the situation at hand, and its relative importance in your life, what is the most positive outcome you can envision, and what would it take to make it a reality? Once you're clear about that, you're ready to take action – even if that action is deciding to just let the disappointment go.

5. Get Involved

Okay, you've decided what you want to do and you're doing it. Now it's time to get your mind off yourself. The fact is, whatever has gone wrong in your life, there still are people who could use your help.

So go help somebody out. Giving help to someone who needs it is one of the most reliable and lasting ways to feel good.

2
GRATITUDE

Be grateful for every hour, and accept what it brings.

Henry David Thoreau

The Nun Study

For nearly two decades now, researchers have been studying the lives of a group of women who became nuns in the 1930's and 1940's. Their findings have enhanced scientists' understanding of subjects from Alzheimer's disease to the benefits of exercise. But one of their most striking findings has to do with happiness and longevity.

When these women became nuns many decades ago, each of them wrote an autobiographical sketch about her life to that point. The researchers assessed those mini-autobiographies for the frequency with which the young nuns expressed positive emotions such as happiness, gratitude, and joy. And what they found was remarkable.

The women who expressed the greatest happiness *in*

their twenties were two and a half times as likely to live to age 85, and *five times as likely to live to age 94.*

Here are the remarkable details. Of the women who most frequently expressed positive emotions in their youthful autobiographies, 90% were still alive at age 85, compared to only 34% of the women who expressed positive emotions least frequently. Nine years later, 54% of the most positive nuns were still alive, as compared to only 11% of the least positive.

How to Have What They're Having

So how can we be more like the nuns with the long, happy lives? As we've already seen, there are a lot of wonderful ways to enhance our happiness. We can spend more of our time doing things we enjoy with people we love. We can develop our strengths and progress toward personally meaningful goals. We can get regular exercise, seek out ways to help others, and learn new things.

But if you have only five minutes a day to dedicate to becoming a happier person, here's how you should spend it.

This evening, sometime before you go to bed, write down five things you feel grateful for.

You might list your spouse's sense of humor, the picture your child drew for you, the strawberry cheesecake ice cream you had for dessert, the encouraging words of a colleague, and your ongoing recovery from an injury.

Each item can just be a few words if you'd like – or even a single word. But as you write your list, take a quiet moment with each item on it. Use that moment to call up a picture in your mind and to experience your gratitude in a heartfelt way.

That's it. Do it again tomorrow night and every night after that. If you feel grateful for some of the same people and things night after night, it's fine to list them again. Just call up a different image in your mind each time and be sure to spend a moment feeling those good feelings of gratitude specific to each item on your list.

Why It Works

How can just five minutes have a real impact on our happiness and well-being? Well, the research shows that the habit of listing what we're grateful for affects us not only while we're making the list, but for the rest of the day as well.

That's the magic of the practice. Knowing that we're going to be listing things we're grateful for in the evening causes us to pay more attention during the day, looking for things to appreciate and noticing the things we feel happy about, and thereby experiencing more positive feelings all day long.

The key is to make it into a regular practice so that every day, even when we aren't thinking about it, our minds are on the lookout for reasons for us to feel happy.

So make a commitment to spend five minutes every evening. You're sure to enjoy the time you spend experiencing your gratitude for the people and things that make you happy. And if you do it every night, it can have a profound effect on your happiness and well-being, and even on how long you're here to enjoy them.

3
HOPE AND PERSISTENCE

Courage does not always roar. Sometimes it is the quiet voice at the end of the day saying, "I'll try again tomorrow."

Mary Anne Radmacher

The Importance of Words

The things we say, whether out loud or to ourselves, have a profound effect not only on how we feel, but also on what we do.

When we tell ourselves *"I can't do it"* or *"They'll never allow it,"* we undermine our own power and motivation to make change in our lives.

When we tell ourselves *"I'll find a way"* or ask *"What haven't I tried yet?"* we give ourselves a feeling of hope that can help us to sustain the persistent effort we need to make things happen.

So it's important that we pay attention to what we say.

Ask yourself this: How often are my comments positive and empowering, and how often are they negative and self-defeating?

If you can shift that balance, even a little, you can have a real impact on how you feel and what you do.

Here's how to start the shift. If you find yourself saying things that suggest that the quality of your life is out of your hands, see if you can find a way to turn them around. One simple way is to use one of my favorite words: "Yet".

The Magic of "Yet"

Adding "yet" to the end of a sentence can turn it from an old complaint into a new challenge. It can remind us how much power we do have, help us set goals for the future, and open us up to finding new ways to achieve them.

It's one of the surest and simplest ways to strengthen our hope and persistence – two essential elements of a happy and successful life.

Here are some examples of the power of "yet."

For Ourselves

*I haven't been able to lose a single pound . . . **yet.***

*I can't get promoted because I'm just not good at giving presentations . . . **yet.***

*I have no idea how I'm going to afford to pay for college . . . **yet.***

For Our Kids

*I just don't understand Algebra . . . **yet.***

*I don't have any friends at my new school . . . **yet.***

*I'm not having a good soccer season . . . **yet.***

In Our Relationships

*I haven't been on a single date since my divorce . . . **yet.***

*I haven't forgiven my sister for that old insult . . . **yet.***

*My spouse doesn't understand how much we need a weekend alone together . . . **yet.***

See the magic? Okay, time to add your own examples to the list. Think up a few ways you can use the power of "yet" to turn complaints into goals in your own life, and to help you sustain the hope and persistence you need to achieve them.

4
KINDNESS

There's no such thing as a small act of kindness.
Every act creates a ripple with no logical end.

Scott Adams

The Power of Kindness

Think of the kindest person you know. Now think of the happiest.

Is it the same person? Chances are good that it is, because very few things make us as happy as being kind. And of course being happier makes us kinder in turn. It's a self-reinforcing cycle that we all want to be a part of.

And that's not just our mothers talking. Research bears it out. In fact, the research suggests that being kind in sustained (and sometimes inconvenient) ways may make us happiest of all.

For example, in a study on the effect of committed volunteering, a group of people with Multiple Sclerosis volunteered and trained to provide peer support to others who also had MS. Over the course of three months, the volunteers made supportive weekly phone calls to the people they were assigned to support. The individuals on both sides of these support calls clearly benefited from them, with both the volunteers and the clients reporting feeling happier than they had before the program began.

So it was good for everyone. But who do you suppose benefited the most?

You probably won't be surprised to hear that it was the volunteers, but you might not be able to guess the magnitude of the difference. In this small study, the clients benefited significantly, but the volunteers benefited profoundly – on average, seven times as much as the people they were assigned to help.

The volunteers reported reduced depression and a greater sense of self-worth, mastery, and self control. Making a significant and sustained effort to help others had a powerfully positive effect on their lives.

But of course it doesn't have to take a structured commitment of this type to get a happiness boost from being kind. Studies have shown improvements in well-being from many different ways of practicing kindness. In one, participants reported feeling significantly happier after conducting five small acts of kindness in a week, especially if they conducted all five of them in a single day.

There's just no doubt about it – being kind makes us happy. Here are a few of the reasons – and some thoughts on how to best appreciate the happiness that kindness brings.

Kindness Improves Our Relationships

More than anything else, kindness strengthens our relationships with our friends and families. And being kind to people outside our closest circles makes us feel more connected to our communities and the people in them.

Kindness Strengthens Our Self-Image

Being kind to others makes us feel good about ourselves – kinder, of course, but also more confident, useful, and in control. *("Here's something I can do to make the world a better place.")* And that good feeling can be reinforced by a double dose of gratitude – *from* the people we're helping, and *for* our own good fortune.

Kindness Creates Meaning

Practicing kindness, especially when we take on a specific, sustained commitment to helping others, enhances our sense of meaning and purpose, which is a key element of a happy life. In fact, a sense of meaning has been shown to enhance virtually every aspect of our well-being – increasing happiness, health, and resilience while reducing anxiety and depression.

Kindness Takes Our Minds Off Ourselves

One of the most common stumbling blocks to happiness is

what psychologists call rumination, or overthinking – brooding over the causes of our problems and the potential outcomes of our worries. It's a habit that negatively affects not only our moods, but also our motivation, concentration and confidence. And one of the surest ways to break the cycle of overthinking is to actively turn our attention away from ourselves by going out of our way to do something kind for someone else.

Kindness Makes It a Better World – And One We Feel Better About

It's simply true that what we put into the world affects what we get back from it. Kindness to others generates kindness in return. In fact, people who are in the habit of practicing kindness consistently rate other people as kinder, their communities as more supportive, and the world as a better place to live, than people who take fewer kind actions toward others.

So how can we make the most of the happiness that kindness brings?

Well, to quote something my mother said often while raising seven kids: "If you're going to be nice, be nice all the way." Practicing kindness with an open heart, appreciating that the gifts we receive are at least as great as the gifts we give, and willingly accepting offers of kindness from others, all will help us to create greater happiness in our lives and the lives of those around us.

5
EXERCISE

*My grandmother started walking five miles a day
when she was sixty. She's ninety-seven now,
and we don't know where the heck she is.*

Ellen DeGeneres

Why We Stay Put

It's not news that getting regular physical exercise is one of the best things we can do for ourselves. It keeps us fit, prevents chronic disease, and extends life. Nearly every day, there are headlines reminding us of its long-term benefits.

But as it turns, out, this emphasis on long-term benefits doesn't provide sufficient motivation for most of us to actually go out and get the regular exercise we need. When we weigh the immediate, concrete inconvenience and discomfort of getting up and exercising *right now* against the future, somewhat-less-than-100%-certain health problems of staying put, the short-term wins all too often. It's just the way we're wired.

Exercise and Mood: The Immediate Payoff

That's why the research on exercise and mood is such good news.

The fact is that we don't have to wait for better heart health or longer lives to benefit from exercise. Working up a sweat is almost certain to make us feel happier right away.

In fact, exercise is one of the most reliable ways to feel good fast, and to sustain that good feeling. Here's why.

More of the Good Stuff

Exercise stimulates the brain to release endorphins, chemicals commonly referred to as pleasure hormones. These are the same hormones that are released when we do something we love to do, and they make us feel happy. So even if we don't always enjoy the exercise itself, our endorphin-loving brains make sure we feel great about doing it.

Less of the Bad Stuff

In addition to stimulating the release of endorphins, exercise also burns cortisol, a chemical often referred to as the stress hormone. Our bodies produce cortisol when we're angry, anxious, or afraid. Exercise is one of the most effective ways to overcome the effects of cortisol and calm back down.

Positive Distraction

When we're stuck in a cycle of negative thoughts or worries, exercise can get our minds off our problems and encourage us to think more broadly about our lives, often leading us to new ideas and solutions.

More Confidence

Setting and meeting challenges, no matter how small, makes us feel good about ourselves. Exercise almost always gives us an immediate sense of accomplishment that can really give a lift to our day.

Finding the Time to Reap the Rewards

Okay, so exercise is going to make us healthier *and* happier. But what if we don't have time to do it? How can we get all of those great benefits if we're just too busy to squeeze it in?

Well, it turns out that exercising makes us more productive and efficient, too – so much so that it more than makes up for the time it takes out of our days.

On days when we exercise, we use our time more efficiently, are mentally sharper and more motivated to work, and are more likely to complete what we set out to do. So no matter how busy we are, it seems that we really do have time to get the emotional and physical benefits of exercise.

And if the prospect of a healthier future isn't always enough to get us out the door, maybe the promise of a happier day today will do the trick.

SECTION TWO
COPE EFFECTIVELY WITH THE NEGATIVE

*Don't wait until you have no more suffering
before allowing yourself to be happy.*

Thich Nhat Hanh

Coping With Sadness, Anger, and Anxiety

You don't need me to tell you that life can be hard. We all face loss, sadness, anxiety, disappointment, and anger – in small ways or large – every day, month, and year.

In fact, happy people experience these so-called negative emotions nearly as often as unhappy people do. The difference is that happy people are able to move fairly easily between negative and positive emotions, and unhappy people tend to get stuck in the negative ones.

So how can we ease that transition for ourselves and avoid getting caught in a downward spiral of negative feelings?

First, we need to *acknowledge and accept* the difficult emotions that we're experiencing. They're a natural reaction to the disappointments, losses, and challenges that life throws our way. If we can stay open to experiencing our feelings, even when it's painful to do so, we'll be much better able to metabolize them and move forward than we would be if we tried to shut them down.

We also need to *consider the causes* of our feelings. If we're angry over a broken promise, worried about our teenager's erratic behavior, or lonely because we've become isolated, we need to pay attention to what our feelings are trying to tell us – that it's time to talk it through, take some action, or make a change.

As we'll see, not every emotion is an accurate reflection of reality. But most are trying to tell us something, and it's worth it to listen for what that something might be.

And finally, we need to *cope effectively* with both our painful feelings and the situations that lead to them. That's what we'll focus on in this section. We'll learn about proven techniques to help us cope with disappointment and anger, effectively challenge our anxiety, and productively solve problems, all while accepting our own humanity and the imperfections that come with it.

6
GAINING PERSPECTIVE

It's not what you look at that matters; it's what you see.

Henry David Thoreau

The Focusing Power of Negative Emotions

Imagine you're heading to your car with your kids after a movie, and laughing about your favorite scene. You're enjoying the beautiful evening and the time with your kids, and thinking in the back of your mind about how much fun you had at the beach with them last week.

Now imagine that a man appearing drunk or unstable suddenly starts yelling threats in your direction while walking quickly toward you. Gone are all thoughts of your vacation, the movie, and the beautiful weather. The only thing that matters to you at that moment is getting your kids into the car, locking the door, and driving safely away.

Which, of course, you successfully do. All is well. And

sorry for the scare.

But what happened back there?

You were having a lovely evening and a threat came out of nowhere. You felt scared for your kids and yourself, and every fiber of your being immediately focused 100% on reacting to the threat. And thank goodness. Continuing to laugh about the movie and enjoy the evening breeze would have been wildly inappropriate given the situation.

The fear narrowed your focus so you could concentrate entirely on dealing with the potential threat. It crowded out everything else that you were seeing, feeling, hearing, and thinking about.

All negative emotions do this to one degree or another – it's just the way we're wired. Fear, worry, disappointment, and anger all narrow our focus to varying degrees, but in essentially the same way. And it isn't usually as helpful as it was in the movie theatre parking lot.

Our Prehistoric Brains

Our species evolved in a situation of scarcity and danger where survival demanded that our ancestors react more strongly to threats than to pleasures. Reacting to a lion on the savannah was a lot more important than enjoying the sunrise. Our brains share many characteristics with those of early humans, but most of us live in vastly different circumstances than they did. As a result, our automatic responses are often out of synch with the situations in which we find ourselves.

So when we're worried about an upcoming performance

review at work, we can focus on the worry to the point where it feeds on itself, increasing our anxiety and offering no benefit in return. When we're disappointed because the review wasn't entirely positive, we can re-live the disappointment again and again, dwelling on our painful feelings instead of figuring out how to resolve the issues. And when we're angry with someone we love, we can brood about what he or she said or did, feeling more and more alienated and ready to fight with every passing hour. In each of these cases, our focus narrows to the point where we see the situation entirely through the lens of our negative emotions and are unable to deal constructively with the situation at hand.

Change Your Lens for a New Perspective

So how can we change our perspective in the midst of strong negative emotions? Here's an easy-to-remember method that I've found to be really helpful.

Photographers know that when you change lenses, you can get a very different view of things. So next time negative emotions get you stuck seeing things with a narrow perspective, un-stick it by changing your lens.

Worried? Use the Long Lens

Worried about something that might go wrong? One of the most effective ways to cope with worry is to gain *psychological distance* by imagining ourselves far away from our current circumstances. This technique actually engages areas of our brains that aren't so caught up in our current worries. So create a vivid picture of yourself five years in the future and see if you're still so worried about what's going on in the here and now.

Disappointed? Try a Wide-Angle Lens

Dealing with defeat or disappointment? Take a wider view that includes consideration of possible benefits of the setback. Ask yourself what you might be able to learn from the situation, and how you could constructively use this turn of events to make your life even better.

Angry? Reverse the Lens

Feeling angry with someone who hurt your feelings or let you down? Reverse your perspective and try to see the situation from the other person's point of view. Even try to imagine how his or her perspective could be right – at least in part. Putting yourself into the other person's shoes can help get you ready to talk things over with an open heart.

The Benefits of Perspective

With all three of these lenses, the point isn't to talk yourself out of your feelings, but to get some additional perspective so you can see the situation more clearly and begin to move forward in a productive way.

So next time negative emotions narrow your focus to the point where you can't see your way to resolution, take a few deep breaths, swap in a new lens, and see what a difference a new perspective can make.

7
TALKING BACK TO ANXIETY

Worry doesn't empty tomorrow of its sorrow;
it empties today of its strength.

Carrie Ten Boom

Anxiety Feeds on Itself

Anxious feelings can lead to anxious thoughts, which then reinforce the anxious feelings and can fuel a downward spiral of anxiety. (Wow, talk about an anxiety-producing sentence.)

But it doesn't have to be that way.

Researchers have developed an effective way for us to disrupt the spiral by challenging the thoughts that are feeding our anxiety.

Anxiety-driven thoughts are very often irrational. The good news is that they're irrational in some pretty predictable ways, so we can learn to recognize and refute them.

Cognitive psychologists have found that engaging in a process of identifying and disputing irrational thoughts is a very effective way to short-circuit the anxiety cycle so we can regain our equilibrium, think more clearly, and feel a lot better.

Short-circuit the anxiety spiral by walking yourself through these three steps.

1. **Recognize your anxiety.** Remind yourself that anxiety naturally fuels irrational thoughts that then reinforce the anxiety. Ask yourself if that's happening to you.

2. **Identify the anxiety-driven thoughts**. *"I'm telling myself that I know the doctor is going to give me bad news. That sounds like my anxiety talking."*

3. **Challenge the faulty reasoning.** *"Do I really have enough evidence to be so sure? What are some of the other possibilities?"*

That's it. And once you've done it, turn your attention to something else. It doesn't matter if it's something fun, something difficult, or something active – just do something that occupies your mind with thoughts other than the ones being fueled by your anxiety. And if those anxious thoughts return, there's no need to feel defeated. Just repeat the process as often as you need to.

Seems pretty simple, right? The trick here is consistency. The more often we go through the process of identifying and disputing irrational, anxiety-fueling thoughts, the easier it will get and the more effective it will become.

Here are some of the most common anxiety-fueled thought patterns, plus some specific ways you can recognize and dispute them. If some of these sound familiar to you, put them into your mental tool kit so you can take them out when you need them.

FORTUNE TELLING
Making Dire Predictions as if They're Facts

If you're telling yourself:

"I know my sales pitch is going to go badly."

"I'm sure she won't want to go out with me."

Stop and ask yourself:

Can I really predict the future, or is this my anxiety talking?

What are some other possible outcomes?

What's one thing I can do to increase my chances of success?

EMOTIONAL REASONING
Treating Anxiety as a Reliable Guide

If you're telling yourself:

"I'm feeling really anxious and uncomfortable. That means this isn't going well."

Stop and ask yourself:

Is my anxiety level always a good gauge of how things are really going?

Do things ever turn out to have gone better than I thought they were going at the time?

TUNNEL VISION
Seeing Only the Negative

If you're telling yourself:

"One of the people in the audience is checking his watch. I'm failing up here."

"I forgot to chill the white wine. The party is ruined."

Stop and ask yourself:

Is my anxiety causing me to ignore anything important?

What do things look like if I expand my perspective and try to see the whole picture?

What can I focus on that is going well?

OVERGENERALIZING
Treating the *Causes* of Disappointment as Permanent and Pervasive

If you're telling yourself:

> *"That was a disaster. I have no talent for it, and I never will."*

Stop and ask yourself:

> Can I think of one specific part of it that went pretty well?

> What strengths and resources do I have that I can use to build on that one pretty good part so it goes even better next time?

CATASTROPHIZING
Treating the *Outcome* of a Disappointment as Permanent and Pervasive

If you're telling yourself:

> *"Now I'll never get a promotion. I'll be lucky if I keep my job."*

> *"She turned me down. I might as well give up. Nobody is ever going to want to go out with me."*

Stop and ask yourself:

> Is it possible that my anxiety is causing me to over-react?

> Is this one event really powerful enough to

determine the course of the rest of my life?

If your anxious thoughts don't quite fit into any of these categories, don't worry. The important thing is that you notice the specific irrational thoughts that are fueling your own anxiety, and dispute them any way you can, even with a simple: "That's not reality. That's my anxiety talking."

The key to success with this process is to practice it consistently and keep doing it over the long term. If you do, you can have a significant impact on your thoughts, your anxiety, and the quality of your life.

8
SOLVING PROBLEMS

Logic can take you from A to B.
Imagination can take you anywhere.

Albert Einstein

Our Natural Problem Focus

Having maxed out her credit cards when she was unemployed last year, Michelle sometimes wakes up in the middle of the night worrying about how she's going to pay her bills.

And now that she's found a new job, she often finds herself distracted at work, justifiably angry and upset that someone who works so hard could find herself in debt over her head.

Michelle spends a lot of time thinking about her problem. But all that thinking doesn't seem to help – she hasn't been able to come up with an effective plan to solve it.

And she's not the only one.

When we have a particularly upsetting problem, most of us find ourselves coming back to it over and over again, fretting over what caused it, or how unfair it is, or how much worse it might get – trying to get to the bottom of it, but remaining stuck with the problem no matter how much attention we give to it.

Why does this happen? Isn't thinking about a problem the best way to come up with a solution? Don't we have to analyze its causes before we can solve it?

In other words, don't we need to get to the bottom of things?

As it turns out, not usually.

Focusing on a problem, especially an emotionally fraught one, is in fact counterproductive in most cases. Our brains see problems as threats, and as we've seen, when our brains are faced with threats, they narrow our thinking to sharpen our attention.

That can be useful when the threat is coming from a snake underfoot or an approaching wildfire. But the solutions to most problems of modern life are more nuanced than running away from snakes and fires. And narrow thinking is usually the opposite of what we need when we have a tough problem to solve.

Switch to a Solution Focus

What we need to do instead is to turn our attention away from the problem – and toward possible solutions. Here's how.

First, Ask Yourself This Question

If I woke up tomorrow and this problem was gone – if it was completely resolved – what would that look like?

Spend a few moments imagining what the complete absence of the problem would look like in as much detail as you can. What would your days be like – in the morning, the afternoon, and the evening? How would you feel, what stresses would be eliminated, what pleasures would you pursue – in short, how would life would be different than it is now?

Next, Turn Your Image into a Story

Staying with the image you just conjured up, create a narrative of what happened to get you from life as it is now to life as it is in your image. If, like Michelle, you're imagining yourself out of debt, how did you accomplish it? If you're imagining yourself more healthy and fit, or in a better relationship with your spouse, what had to take place for those things to happen? Construct a story about what the road might look like from where you are now to where you want to be.

Now Begin Your Journey Down That Road

Choose one or two of the elements of your story that you can act on, and get started on them. Your vision of life free from the problem will serve as your goal, and your story of the journey will be your road map to achieving it. Once you begin to make progress, you'll be able to develop an even clearer picture of both your goal and your road map, so stay open to the lessons your journey has to teach about where you want to go and how you choose to get there.

Problems are a part of life, and not every one can be solved – but most can be. It may not be easy, and it may not be fast. But if there is a problem weighing you down, chances are very good that you can find a way to resolve it if you start thinking not about where you are or how you got there, but about where you want to go.

9

PRACTICING SELF-COMPASSION

The ultimate lesson that we all have to learn is unconditional love, which includes not only others, but ourselves as well.

Elisabeth Kubler-Ross

Chocolate Peanut Butter Pie

Think of someone you really love who's been working hard to achieve something, maybe a friend who's made a commitment to lose weight and live a healthier life. She's been making good progress by eating right most of the time and getting a lot of exercise.

Now imagine that the two of you have gone out to dinner to celebrate a special occasion, and she orders the restaurant's famous chocolate peanut butter pie for dessert.

How do you react?

Do you:

> A. Smile and hope she really enjoys the indulgence, since none of us should feel we have to be disciplined all the time.

> B. Tell her she should be ashamed of her lack of will power and that she might as well go ahead and finish sabotaging her efforts by eating a whole bag of Oreos when she gets home.

Okay, that was the easy question. I know you're a kind and supportive friend and you'd never act the way I described in option B.

Now here's the harder one.

What if the person ordering the dessert wasn't your friend? What if it was you?

Do you ever talk to yourself in that *"you are just hopeless"* tone of voice? Or even if you wouldn't actually talk that way to yourself, do you find yourself being less understanding of your own imperfections than you are of your loved ones? If so, you're not alone. Most of us are our own worst critics.

Why are we so hard on ourselves? Dr. Kristen Neff, a professor of psychology at the University of Texas, says the main reason is that we're afraid that if we are *"too soft"* on ourselves, we'll let ourselves get away with anything. *"In other words,"* she says, we *"confuse self-compassion with self-indulgence."*

The Surprising Truth about Self-Compassion and Responsibility

It's easy to understand why we'd confuse the two. After all, I'm not responsible for my friend's behavior, but I am responsible for my own. If I treat myself with compassion, don't I risk just giving up and letting it all go to pieces?

Well, no. In fact, it's just the opposite.

Research clearly demonstrates that people who treat themselves with self-compassion rather than self-criticism take greater responsibility for their mistakes and are more motivated to try again after failure. They're better able to admit to their flaws and make improvements because they can look clearly at themselves without fear of excessive self-criticism. As a result, they're less depressed and anxious, have greater confidence in their abilities, and are less upset when things don't go well.

Practicing self-compassion can help people quit smoking and stick with healthy eating and exercise programs. And it can help us recover from painful experiences. For example, researchers have found that newly divorced people who make a point of speaking compassionately toward themselves cope more successfully with their new circumstances and emerge from their divorces with greater self-esteem and optimism for the future.

Three Ways to Become More Self-Compassionate

Ready to develop a habit of treating yourself with greater compassion? Here are three ways to get started.

1. Treat Yourself as You Would Treat a Loved One

The essence of self-compassion is treating yourself with the same loving care and kindness you would offer a friend or loved one. So if you find that you're being harsh toward yourself, ask how you would treat someone else you care about in that same situation.

Let's stick with the divorce example for a minute. Say you're going through a tough divorce. To practice self-compassion, ask yourself what you would say and do if the person going through the divorce was your sister instead. You wouldn't ask her again and again how she could have failed at the most important relationship in her life. You'd comfort her, remind her that you love her, and help her to remember the strengths that she can use to get through the rough times and thrive again.

Or if your good friend lost his job, you wouldn't tell him he's washed up and useless. You'd encourage him, remind him of his terrific skills and abilities, and help him get emotionally prepared to go back into the job market or train for a new career.

2. Ask for Support

How often have you told friends that you wished they had let you know when they needed some encouragement or support? Often, the most compassionate thing we can do for ourselves is to let the people who love us know we're feeling down and need a friend to listen. So go ahead – ask for what you need.

3. Act Compassionately Toward Others

One of the best ways to cultivate compassion toward ourselves is to practice compassion toward others. Helping people in need reminds us that we're all in this together, that life never promised to be perfect or even easy, and that the best response to anyone's pain – including our own – is kindness and compassion.

SECTION THREE
DEVELOP STRONG RELATIONSHIPS

Being deeply loved by someone gives you strength,
while loving someone deeply gives you courage.

Lao Tzu

What Do the Happiest People Have in Common?

Imagine this.

You're a contestant on a game show, and you're up for the big prize. (It's your imagination, so you get to dream up any prize you'd like.)

The host brings onto the stage three people you don't know and tells you that your challenge is to sort these strangers according to how happy they are on the basis of their answers to a single question.

You get to choose the question, but you have to ask each of the three people the same one.

What question would you ask?

Here are some choices:

1. How big is your bank account?

2. How strong are your personal relationships?

3. How meaningful do you find your work?

4. How optimistic are you?

5. How often do you feed sad?

(Cue theme music.)

Okay, contestant, your time is up. Which of these five questions do you choose?

I'm guessing you were able to eliminate Question #1 pretty quickly. Having a certain level of income is essential to happiness and well-being, but beyond that, having more and more money makes less and less of a difference.

Were you also able to eliminate Question #5? As we've seen throughout this book, happiness is not the absence of sadness. Very happy people experience sad feelings pretty regularly in their lives. They're just less likely to remain stuck in those feelings than less happy people are.

The other three options are all reasonable choices.

Personal relationships, meaningful work (whether paid or volunteer, at home or out in the world), and an optimistic outlook are all very important elements of our happiness.

But you only get to ask each of the three individuals one question. So which is of these factors is in fact the strongest predictor of happiness?

Are you ready for the answer? The best question to ask is Question #2: How strong are your personal relationships?

When researchers study very happy people, they find that *many* of them do work that they find meaningful, and *most* of them have highly optimistic outlooks. But virtually *all* of them have strong personal relationships.

To be more specific, very happy people generally have at least three close, healthy relationships. One may or may not be with a partner or spouse; single people can be every bit as happy as those who are part of a couple. Others may be with family members, friends of long-standing, or even relatively new friends with whom they've quickly developed strong bonds.

These are the people who celebrate our good fortune, help us through hard times, and make good times even better. They give us advice and encouragement, support our dreams, and laugh at our jokes. We enjoy being with them, and we feel good knowing that we can count on them and that they can count on us in return.

These are the people we love, and who love us back. And

they are the people who make us happy.

So how can we nurture our relationships with them, so that we – and they – can be at our happiest? That's just what we'll cover in this section.

10
WHAT THE HAPPIEST
COUPLES DO

Love comforts like sunshine after rain.

Unknown

Research That Changes Lives

Do you remember hearing some years ago about an academic researcher in Seattle who was able to predict with 94% accuracy which marriages would fail, just by watching a single very brief interaction between the spouses? It may have seemed hard to believe, but Dr. John Gottman had the research to back up his claim.

Impressive, to be sure. The best part of the story, though, is what happened next.

Dr. Gottman realized that being able to predict which marriages would fail wasn't all that helpful in his work with couples who wanted their marriages to thrive. For that, he had to turn his attention to studying couples in truly successful marriages and documenting just what it is that they do that makes their relationships work so well.

What Dr. Gottman learned from that research can help us all to build, nurture, and even repair relationships with our spouses or partners, and even with our children and friends.

So here it is – a summary of what couples in the very best marriages do to make their relationships thrive. If you have a spouse or partner, why not talk about which of these things you already do, and then choose some new ones to work on together?

Strive for a 5:1 Ratio

In their interactions with each other, the happiest couples average five positive comments for every negative one. Keep track for a day or two and see how close you come to that ratio. If you're down around 3:1 or maybe even 1:1, which is really very common, then this is the single best place to put your first efforts toward improving your relationship.

Turn Toward Each Other

Dr. Gottman says that close relationships consist of a series of *"emotional bids"* in which one partner reaches out to the other with a comment, question, or touch. In the healthiest relationships, partners consistently respond to such bids by emotionally or physically *"turning toward each other"* to show that they are open, listening, and engaged. In unhealthy relationships, partners often ignore emotional bids or react to them with anger or hostility.

Be Open to Influence

Do you feel like your partner is open to being persuaded by your point of view, or stubbornly determined not to be influenced by what you have to say? It's easy to get into a habit of always sticking to our own positions, but that's a trap that people in the most successful marriages take care to avoid.

Spend Enjoyable Time Together

This, after all, is how (and why) we begin relationships in the first place, so why do we think we can sustain them without it? The fact is, though, that as life crowds in, it's all too easy to give up time together in favor of work, parenting, or just catching up on our sleep. But giving it up comes at a real cost. Cliché or not, setting aside regular time to enjoy being together is one of the essential elements of the happiest relationships.

Make the Most of Conflict

Conflict is essential to healthy relationships. No two people are aligned on all things at all times, so relationships with no conflict are almost certainly ones in which at least one person is sometimes suppressing his or her true feelings and needs.

And conflict need not be destructive. In fact, Dr. Gottman has observed that well-managed conflict actually serves to bring close couples closer over time, as the partners express their honest hurts and disagreements and work together toward positive resolution. Here's how they do it.

Introduce Conflict Gently

When you bring up a problem or complaint, do it without criticizing or insulting your partner. *"Honey, I feel frustrated that you called me to pick up the kids when you knew I needed to catch up at work"* gets a conversation off to a much better start than *"Why are you so selfish all the time?"*

Avoid Contempt, Insults, and Hostility

Okay, this came from Dr. Gottman's research into failing marriages, not successful ones, but it's worth pointing out here anyway. Contempt, insults, and hostility destroy relationships; it's as simple as that. Don't fall into their trap.

Repair the Conversation

When couples in the strongest relationships argue, they take steps to de-escalate the negative feelings that can arise as they go along. They might apologize for a painful remark, inject a bit of well-intentioned humor, or just offer each other a sympathetic smile. All of these small repairs can remind both partners that they're fundamentally on each other's side so they can let their defenses down a bit and try to work things out.

I, for one, am grateful that Dr. Gottman turned his attention from researching what makes marriages fail to studying what makes the best ones thrive. The quality of our close relationships is by far the strongest contributor to our overall happiness, so learning what works and taking even one or two steps to improve our most important relationships can have a profound effect on the quality of our lives.

11
THE SURPRISING TRUTH ABOUT EXTROVERSION

*Eeyore, you can't stay in your corner of the forest
waiting for others to come to you. You have to
go to them sometimes.*

A.A. Milne

Surprising Research, With the Ring of Truth

I'm no Eeyore, but I do consider myself a bit of an introvert.

I really enjoy doing quiet things like reading, writing, and going for long walks by myself, and I can feel a little shy around people I don't know.

But I'm also determined to live the best life I can. And there's a lot of convincing research showing that extroverts – people who are not only highly social, but also bold, novelty-seeking, and energetically engaged with life – are happier than introverts. They generally enjoy their lives more in the short term and are more satisfied with their lives over the long term.

So what's an introvert to do? We are who we are, right?

Well, that's the surprising part.

It turns out that extroverts aren't happy simply because of *who they are* – they're happy because of *what they do*. And doing the things extroverts do – seeking out social situations, taking on leadership roles, trying out new experiences – actually makes all of us happier, whether we are "by nature" extroverts, introverts, or somewhere in between.

To put it another way, virtually all of us are actually happier when we act like extroverts.

Yes, you read that right. Even people who have a natural tendency to avoid social situations, stay in the background, and stick with what we know are happier when we're being social, putting ourselves forward, and trying out new experiences.

Surprising though it is, I have to say that I find this research entirely convincing. After all, I may sort of dread parties, but I usually wind up enjoying myself when I go to them. I may wish I hadn't scheduled that lunch with a friend, but I know I'm going to have a wonderful time anyway. And I may love going to the same few places for vacations, but when we try out someplace new, I'm always thrilled that we did.

I don't at all mean to suggest that we should throw off our natures and pretend to be people we're not.

I'd never consider giving up the pleasures of a good

book or a solitary walk. In fact, I not only enjoy these pleasures, I really value and need them – especially when I've been out in the world acting like an extrovert.

But I'm taking this lesson to heart. I'm convinced that more energetically engaging with life – being more social, taking more chances, and trying more new things – will make me even happier than I already am. I'm going to do it, and I'll bet I'm going to love it.

And then I'm going to go home and read a book.

12
THE ART OF LISTENING

Courage is what it takes to stand up and speak.
Courage is also what it takes to sit down and listen.

Winston Churchill

Relationships and Listening

Have you ever been talking with a friend about a problem and found her jumping in with solutions when what you really wanted her to do was listen?

Do you and your spouse ever revisit the same argument over and over again without either of you feeling like the other person is really hearing your point of view?

The friends we value the most are the ones who really listen when we need them to. And the strongest relationships are the ones in which both people feel they are being heard. In this chapter, we'll look at how to be a great listener, and to make sure you get your turn to be *listened to*.

How to Be a Great Listener

Great listening is a gift of the heart and the mind. Here's how to give it.

Focus

Ignore distractions. Close the laptop, silence the phone, turn off the TV, and just listen.

Empathize

Put yourself in the other person's shoes and try to really understand his or her experience and perspective.

Stay in the Moment

Don't rehearse what you're going to say in response. (That's not listening; that's talking inside of your head.)

Clarify

Occasionally ask brief questions to enhance your understanding of the speaker's meaning, or repeat back what you think you heard and ask if you've understood it correctly. Then really listen to the response.

Be Open-Minded

Try to resist forming opinions, especially before you've heard the other person out.

Respond

Now that you've really listened, go ahead and offer to share your opinion or an experience you've had that might shed some light on the situation. Once we feel that we've really been listened to, we're better able to hear and build on others' ideas in ways that are right for us.

How to Really Be Heard

Of course, you don't only want to listen well – you also want to be heard. And for the sake of your relationships, it's important that you know you *will* be heard.

In fact, it's so important that it's worth it to be very deliberate about taking turns listening and being listened to, especially in the case of a conflict with strong feelings on both sides. In a case such as that, here's what I recommend you do.

Have a look together through the principles of being a great listener, then set a timer for ten minutes. During those ten minutes, one of you will speak while the other really listens. At the end of the ten minutes, set the timer again while the other person does the listening.

If you're the second person to speak, try not to focus primarily on responding to what the other person said. Concentrate instead on sharing your own experience, feelings, and perspective.

After a round or two of taking turns, you'll probably have a much better appreciation of each other's point of view and will be ready to have a good, unstructured conversation.

This process of taking turns may feel a little contrived at first, but it's been shown to work very well, and I find that listening and knowing I'll be listened to in turn feels so good that any awkwardness dissipates almost as soon as I begin.

So go ahead and try it – it's worth the effort. After all, the quality of our relationships is influenced dramatically by the nature of our conversations. Really taking the time to listen to each other is one of the best gifts we can give – both to ourselves and to the people we love.

13
THE POWER OF FORGIVENESS

*Getting over a painful experience is much like
crossing monkey bars. You have to let go
at some point in order to move forward.*

C.S. Lewis

Freedom to Move Forward

Forgiving others has been shown to enhance our happiness, improve our relationships, and have immediate and lasting effects on our physical health and well-being. It also gives us the freedom to move forward in our lives rather than being stuck holding grudges from the past.

Researchers who study forgiveness define it as a conscious decision to let go of ill-will toward someone who has wronged you. In other words, it's a choice to move beyond hoping that someone who hurt you gets the suffering or other bad consequences you feel that he or she deserves.

Some Reasonable Objections

As healthy as practicing forgiveness may be, it can run counter to some entirely reasonable objections. Let's take a look at a few.

I can't excuse it.

Okay. Forgiving doesn't mean that you need to minimize or excuse what's been done or how it's made you feel. In fact, forgiving can allow you to focus on healing the harm done to you without being distracted by a desire for revenge or a feeling of ill-will toward the other person.

It's not fair.

That's true. Extending forgiveness to someone who doesn't deserve it *isn't* fair. It's much easier to forgive someone who apologizes and makes amends. And perhaps the person you forgive will do so. If you're to have a healthy ongoing relationship, it will certainly be much better if the person does. But if you make that a precondition of your own decision to forgive, you run a real risk of never forgiving. And remember, you're forgiving for the sake of your own health and happiness, so you really don't want to set up conditions that will prevent it.

This person is bad for me.

Strong connections with other people are what make us happiest in life, so you don't want to end relationships over petty hurts. But sometimes you really do need to break things off entirely with people who are not good for you.

Fortunately, you can still get the benefits of forgiving. Forgiveness doesn't require you to reconcile with the person you're forgiving. You can choose to let go of ill-will toward someone without choosing to continue your relationship. You don't even have to extend the relationship long enough to let the person know about your forgiveness if doing so would be unhealthy for you.

How to Do It

Forgiving can be hard to do. But it gets easier with practice, and there are some good strategies that have been proven to help. So if you're struggling to let go of a grudge, some of these techniques are almost sure to make it easier.

Remember a time someone forgave you even though you didn't entirely deserve it.

We've all been the beneficiaries of other people deciding to treat us with more mercy than justice. Recalling how being forgiven felt to you can help you to get past the "It isn't fair" objection.

Think of something you value, or valued, about the person who's wronged you.

The point isn't to justify the bad behavior, just to remind yourself that he or she is a human being with both strengths and weaknesses.

Imagine forgiving the person, and picture letting him or her know.

What would you say? How might the other person respond? How might he or she try to explain? Imagining this conversation can help you see things from the other person's perspective.

Decide to forgive.

Because forgiving can go against the grain in spite of how healthy it is, you'll need to make a conscious decision to forgive, and to remind yourself of your decision if those feelings of ill-will start to come back.

If you choose to, let the person know you'd like to talk things over.

Let him or her know that you've made the choice to forgive, and explain how you would like to move forward. Don't use this as an opportunity to inflict the punishment you really think the person deserves; instead, simply talk about the experience and your decision to move beyond it.

If You're Not Ready

If you try these steps and keep getting stuck along the way, you may not be ready to forgive just yet. That's okay. Give it some time, then try again and see if you get farther. It's not always easy, but if we take it step by step, we can develop an ability to forgive that will have lasting benefits on our relationships, our health, and our happiness.

SECTION FOUR
PURSUE MEANINGFUL GOALS

*If your success is not on your own terms, if it looks
good to the world but does not feel good
in your heart, it is not success at all.*

Anna Quindlen

Goals and Meaning

One of the key elements of a happy life is making progress toward goals that we find personally meaningful. Goals focus and motivate us. They increase our resilience by giving us reasons to keep going after setbacks. And they give us a highly gratifying sense of purpose, forward motion, and meaning.

We often think of goal pursuit as a tradeoff in which we willingly reduce our happiness in the short term in exchange for greater happiness in the end. But in fact, when we pursue well-chosen goals, progressing toward them actually increases our happiness even more than achieving them does. Even when the work involved is difficult, uncomfortable, or inconvenient, the knowledge that we're making progress toward goals that genuinely matter to us can dramatically increase our current sense of well-being.

So it's important that we choose our goals well. Pursuing them doesn't have to be easy or entirely pleasant. In fact, we gain the most happiness from working toward goals that demand a lot from us. But they do need to fit well with who we are and what we value.

In this section, we'll begin by reflecting on our lives and setting some personally meaningful goals. Then we'll learn about the most effective, research-tested techniques for pursuing, sticking with, and achieving them – in ways that will enhance our lives along the journey, as well as when we reach the destination.

14
SETTING GOALS

You rarely have time for everything you want in this life,
so you need to make choices. And hopefully, your choices
can come from a deep sense of who you are.

Fred Rogers

Taking Stock

Most of the time, our lives proceed at such speed that we
don't have much of a chance to reflect on them – to consider
our sources of happiness and meaning, our relationships, our
everyday pleasures and concerns, and our sense of balance.

This chapter is a chance to do just that.

Following are six areas that contribute powerfully to the
quality of our lives. Some are the subjects of the sections of
this book, and others are somewhat more specific. Start by
considering each of them in relation to your own life and
giving each one a rating from 1 – 5, with 1 signifying real

dissatisfaction with that area and 5 signifying great satisfaction.

Connections with Others

As we've seen, the quality of our relationships with others has a far greater impact on the quality of our lives than does any other single factor.

So think about the relationships that are most important to you. Do they get the time and attention they need to thrive? Are they more a source of energy and joy or of frustration and unproductive conflict?

Emotional Well-Being

Our emotional states are profoundly important to our happiness. In fact, our emotional responses to events have a much greater impact on how we experience our lives than do the events themselves.

Take a few minutes to consider the state of your emotional well-being. Do you generally feel pretty confident and optimistic or more anxious and discouraged? How much do you enjoy the good things in your life, and how well do you cope with negative feelings and experiences? Are you generally kind to yourself or more often critical?

Physical Well-Being

Some people like exercising and some people don't, but the fact is that – whether or not we enjoy it – almost all of us are happier and healthier when we find a way to make regular exercise a part of our lives.

How is this area working in your life? Hard one or easy? Going well or not so well?

Work and Accomplishment

Whether we're employees, volunteers, parents, entrepreneurs, or students, doing satisfying work can give our lives purpose and structure, and increase our self-confidence in the present and our hope for the future. But of course work can also be frustrating, overwhelming, and unrewarding.

Think about the work that you do – is it more a source of satisfaction or frustration? Is it in synch with what you're good at, what you value, and what you enjoy doing? And how about the amount of time you spend doing it – does it feel in balance or does it overwhelm other things that are important to you?

Sense of Purpose and Meaning

Simply put, we're happiest with our lives when they feel purposeful and filled with meaning, whether that meaning comes from helping others, making art, raising a family, building a business or career, experiencing natural beauty, learning new things, or connecting with our religious or spiritual side.

So think about what means the most to you and whether you're happy with the strength of your connection to those important sources of meaning and purpose in your life.

Financial Well-Being

Money can't buy happiness, but financial hardship can certainly make life stressful, whether that hardship comes from real poverty or from the strain of spending more than we earn regardless of our income. Making even slow progress toward financial goals can really enhance our sense of control over our lives, just as getting deeper into debt can add a lot of anxiety.

How are things going for you in this domain of your life?

Considering Changes

Now that you've had a chance to think about and rate each of these areas of your life, go back and look at your high numbers. Take a moment to celebrate these areas of great happiness in your life – think about what you and others do to make them work so well, and appreciate the joy and energy you get from them.

Then have a look at your low numbers. Choose one that's important to you, and consider this question.

Imagine a future in which this area of your life has gone from a source of dissatisfaction to a source of real happiness and energy -- what would that look like?

Try to really give yourself over to imagining how it would look and feel for that area of your life to be going wonderfully well in ways that fit with what you value and enjoy the most.

Now extend that image to include what might have happened to change that area of your life from a source of frustration and anxiety to a source of great energy and joy.

Take successive steps back in time to picture more and more concrete and specific steps that make up a conceivable path toward that wonderful future you imagined. This path is a rich source of practical goals that can make a real difference in your life.

Set Goals

Now begin to set goals that can move your life in the direction you want to take it.

Give yourself a running start by committing to goals that are:

Positive

Frame your goals in terms of what you're moving toward, not what you're getting away from.

"I' going to go back to school and get that degree in art education so I can have the career I really want."

Authentic

For your goals to enhance your happiness, they need to be a good fit with what you love to do, what you value, and where your strengths lie.

"I love to help kids find their talents, and I'm creative and patient."

Practical

Finally, your goals should be in synch with the rest of your aims in life, achievable with hard work and persistence, and flexible enough to allow you to respond in the face of changing circumstances.

Okay, have you committed to some personally meaningful goals? Then let's move on to the next step: Making Progress.

15
MAKING PROGRESS

*Destiny is not a thing to be waited for;
it is a thing to be achieved.*

William Jennings Bryan

The Benefits

Progressing toward goals can help us to improve our lives in the present and look forward to the future with greater optimism and confidence. Plus it feels great. Our brains are hard-wired to enjoy meeting challenges, especially those along the way to the achievement of a goal.

Of course, many goals get abandoned, causing more frustration than optimism, and more self-criticism than self-confidence.

But it doesn't have to be that way. Researchers have learned a lot about how we can best pursue and achieve our goals. Here's some of the best of what they've found.

Give Yourself Permission to Change

When we make changes in our lives, we're generally giving up one set of attitudes and behavior in favor of another. And one of the things that often get in our way is that some of what we value about ourselves is wrapped up in the old attitudes and behavior.

Maybe you're a perfectionist who wants to be easier on yourself, but you value your high standards and don't want to give them up. The trick here is to unbundle the behavior you're seeking to change from the characteristic you prize. Remind yourself that demanding perfection can actually get in the way of positive progress and that you can still seek to do your best while at the same time treating yourself with kindness and compassion.

Unbundle what you want to shed from what you want to keep, and give yourself permission to make the change you seek.

Set Yourself Up for Success

Take steps to set yourself up for success right away – while you're at your most motivated. Commit to a walking schedule with a friend, make a reservation for a special weekend with your spouse, give away the chips in your pantry, or toss your cigarettes and ask your family for support.

Get Started by . . . Starting

Most goals never make it out of the starting gate. We think

we need to wait for circumstances to be just right before we begin, or that we'd better start with something hard to see if we can really do it, or we hold off on beginning because we're afraid of committing to what it will really take.

The truth is that progress feels great and makes us want to do more. So take one joyful step toward your goal and let yourself feel good about having the courage to begin.

Visualize the Journey

I know this doesn't sound nearly as exciting as visualizing the destination, but to really get the thing done, you'll need to focus on what it's going to take. Think through what you'll need to do to achieve your goal, and then picture yourself taking the various steps.

Create an "If . . . Then" Plan

Every goal presents challenges along the way, often just when our commitment and energy are flagging. So the best time to think about how you'll deal with those challenges without getting off track is before they happen.

Think about the challenges you're likely to face and how you can best cope with them, and commit to an "If . . . Then" plan. For example, "If I don't feel like exercising/studying/paying bills, then I'll set a timer and do it for five minutes to see if that gets me in the groove."

Bounce Back After Setbacks

You can't always predict what will go wrong, but you can be sure that some things will. Expect it, experience it, then forgive the universe, yourself, or who or whatever else messed up your plan and find a way to get back on the journey. Remember why you want to go where you're headed, then find your way back to the road, try a new path, or just plow on through the trees.

Enjoy it Along the Way

Remember, the goals that make us the happiest are the ones we enjoy pursuing. And if you don't enjoy the journey, you're not likely to make it to the destination. So remember why you're doing it, take it at a pace you can enjoy, and don't forget to celebrate every time you crest a steep hill, cross a deep ravine, or just get a little farther down the road on a beautiful sunny day.

16
STAYING ON TRACK

It may take a little time to get to where you want to be.
But if you pause and think for a moment, you will
notice that you are no longer where you were.
Do not stop – keep going.

Rodolfo Costa

Through the Slog

Committing to a new goal is exciting, and progress often comes quickly in the early stages. But achieving our goals requires us to stay on track even when things have become a bit of a slog. In this chapter, we'll look at two skills that can help us do just that: gaining psychological distance and overcoming procrastination.

The First Skill: Gaining Psychological Distance

The human brain's default orientation is to focus on our experience in the here and now. Without that natural focus on our immediate experience, we'd never get to work on time or appreciate the feel of the breeze against our skin on a beautiful spring day.

But there can be tremendous benefit to sometimes taking ourselves out of the here and now by imagining ourselves in a different place or time, or by taking on an outsider's perspective. When we do this, we engage different areas of our brains – areas that can be very helpful in keeping us on track toward our goals.

Psychologists refer to this technique as *gaining psychological distance,* and it's as simple as using our imaginations to activate the parts of our brains that aren't so caught up with our immediate experience, perceptions, and feelings.

The Science

There are at least three kinds of psychological distance: *temporal* (distance in time), *spatial* (distance in space) and *personal* (distance in perspective). Research has demonstrated that when we're focused on our experience in the here and now, we tend to base our decisions and actions on short-term wants and needs. But when we step outside of that immediate focus by picturing ourselves at a temporal, spatial, or personal distance, we're better able to base our decisions and actions more on our deeply held values and longer-term goals.

How to Do It

The simple process of picturing ourselves at a distance from our immediate circumstances activates parts of the anterior and dorsal regions of our brains that naturally help us to take the longer view and act more consistently with what's most important to us. Here's how to do it effectively.

Temporal Distance

Imagine it's five years from now. Really picture it – what is your life like, what are you doing, how do you feel? The more fully you can imagine it, the more your brain will be able to help you out.

Spatial Distance

Imagine you're somewhere far away from where you are now. Be sure to choose a specific place and really call up the sights, sounds, and feelings of being there.

Personal Distance

Imagine you're watching yourself at this moment. Create a picture in your mind of what the situation would look like from the perspective of an observer. The point isn't to judge what you see, but simply to try as fully as possible to take on the visual perspective of a neutral third party.

Researchers have found that these three types of psychological distance are pretty interchangeable, so feel free to generate which ever of them comes most naturally to you, or feels most useful in a particular situation.

When to Use It

Really focusing on the here and now is immensely important to fully experiencing and enjoying the pleasures of life. But being able to gain psychological distance can be very helpful in certain situations. Here are three of them.

Making Decisions

When we're in our default here-and-now perspective, we tend to make decisions based on the most *obvious or concrete* features of the alternatives before us. When we take on psychological distance, we're better able to base our decisions on the features that are most *important* to us instead.

Say you've set a goal of making regular contributions to your retirement account. But you also need to replace your old car. You know you won't be able to meet your financial goals if you buy an expensive car, so you decide to go with something basic, safe, and relatively inexpensive.

When you get to the dealer, of course, the sales person will try to re-focus your attention away from safety and affordability to more concrete features like heated seats, extra room, and a DVD player.

Left to its own devices, your brain will be very easily talked into making a decision based on those concrete features that appeal to its here-and-now orientation. So if you want to stay on track toward your financial goals, use one of the techniques to gain psychological distance and engage the parts of your brain that care more about your comfortable retirement than they do about how many cup holders your new car will have.

Resisting Temptation

When we generate psychological distance, we're also able to exercise substantially greater self-control in resisting temptations that can de-rail our progress toward both short-term and long-term goals.

So next time you're fighting temptation, picture yourself in the future, or far away, or as a neutral observer, and you'll be better able to resist. It may not always work at first, but the more consistently you do it, the more powerful the technique will become for you.

Staying Focused

One of the reasons it's so hard to stay committed to long-term goals is that they're so often inconvenient, difficult, or just plain unpleasant in the short term. Gaining psychological distance can help us to keep our eyes on the prize so we don't lose our forward momentum.

Say you've enrolled in a part-time masters program so you can achieve your goal of becoming an art teacher. As excited as you are about your future career, and as enjoyable as you find the subject, the fact is that juggling work, school, and family is really hard to do. So when the time comes to register for yet another semester of classes, your natural here-and-now perspective will tend to focus on the work, the stress, and the expense of sticking with it.

This is a great time to generate some psychological distance, engage your brain's long-term focus, and take action consistent with your determination to prepare for a career you will love.

The Second Skill: Overcoming Procrastination

Another hurdle we all confront in the pursuit of our goals is procrastination. It's a nearly universal challenge, but researchers have developed some proven techniques to help us fight it. And the first step in getting past it is to acknowledge the simple truth of what's going on – that there's something you feel you should be doing that you don't want to do right now.

It isn't a moral failing. It's a completely ordinary human response. Once you acknowledge it in a neutral way, you put yourself in a position to decide what to do about it.

So ask yourself this question: Why don't I want to do this thing right now?

As with much of life, specificity counts. *"Because I'm a lazy procrastinator"* won't get you anywhere. It doesn't offer you a path out of the situation. But if you can be specific about what's going on, then you can take concrete steps to move forward.

Here are some of the most common reasons we procrastinate, and what we can do about them.

Inertia

Inertia is the tendency of an object at rest to stay at rest. And very often, inertia is the simple reason we don't get started on something we feel we should be doing. It can be surprisingly hard to get ourselves going, especially if we're trying to move from doing something passive, like watching TV, to being more actively engaged in an activity – *even if it's an activity we enjoy.*

The Fix

Get inertia on the side of what you need to do. After all, inertia isn't only the tendency of an object at rest to stay at rest. It's also the tendency of an object in motion to stay in motion. So get yourself in motion – there is real magic in simply beginning.

How? Give yourself what I call a *Five Minute Start*. Tell yourself you're going to start with five minutes on the task and then take it from there. Most of the time, inertia will keep you moving.

Avoiding Boredom

Some things that we have to do on the way to achieving a goal are boring, and really, who wants to be bored?

The Fix

Find the most interesting part of what you need to do and start there, even if it isn't the most logical place to begin. Like with the Five Minute Start, once you get going, inertia will likely keep you going.

Anxiety

If you're not sure about your ability to successfully complete a task, you may feel anxious about even beginning it. None of us enjoys anxiety, and it's natural to want to avoid things that cause us to feel it.

The Fix

First, find the part of the task you're most comfortable with and start there. Then, once you've gotten your feet wet, break it down. Divide the task into manageable steps, sketch out how and when you aim to complete each one, and celebrate how good you feel every time you get one step closer to completion.

Gaining psychological distance and overcoming procrastination can help you stay on track until you get your goals across the finish line – well, most of your goals. A few of them are going to need some extra care just to get out of the starting gate.

Let's have a look at how we can achieve goals

that feel so far beyond our reach that we don't quite know how to begin.

17
ACHIEVING YOUR MOST CHALLENGING GOALS

People who say it cannot be done shouldn't interrupt those who are doing it.

George Bernard Shaw

When Goals Feel Out of Reach

Think for a moment about something you really want to achieve, but just don't think you can – something that you've long wished for without ever thinking you could actually accomplish it. Maybe you think of it as a dream rather than a goal, because you just don't see yourself ever being able to make it happen.

Unless it's truly unachievable or out of synch with your values, finding a way to turn that dream into a goal could be of enormous benefit to your happiness and well being.

Maybe you deeply want to go to graduate school and

change careers, but you can't even imagine taking a standardized entrance exam after all these years. Perhaps you'd like to become an accomplished public speaker, but the very idea of getting up before a group fills you with dread. Or maybe you want to run a marathon, but right now you can't quite run around the block.

What can we do when our goals feel this far beyond our reach?

Here's the best way I know to tackle goals that feel out of reach. It starts with three zones of behavior – the Comfort Zone, the Stretch Zone, and the Panic Zone.

The Comfort Zone

The Comfort Zone is where we operate most of the time, doing the things we know how to do in the ways that we're used to doing them. Our comfort zones are essential to living our lives, but not a lot of change happens in them.

The Stretch Zone

The Stretch Zone is where the magic happens. It's outside of our Comfort Zone, but short of our Panic Zone. It's where we can push ourselves to try something out, do something more, or learn something new – where we can stretch our understanding of what's possible for us.

The Panic Zone

The Panic Zone is where we land when we force ourselves to dive head first into the deep end of our most challenging goals. Few of us spend much time actually operating in our

Panic Zones. We may dive into them from time to time, determined to face our fears, but they're such uncomfortable places to be that we usually climb back out pretty quickly.

Finding Your Zone

To make progress toward goals that feel out of reach, we need to consciously choose to spend time in our Stretch Zones.

Let's look at that goal of becoming an accomplished public speaker.

In your Comfort Zone, you may not do any public speaking at all. But if you went all the way to suddenly speaking in front of a large group in a formal setting, you'd be in your Panic Zone.

To create your Stretch Zone, think about ways that you could go beyond your Comfort Zone without feeling so uncomfortable that you retreat right back to where you started. Perhaps you could speak in front of a small group, or a couple of friends, or the mirror.

The trick is to do something that makes you uncomfortable, but doesn't cause flat-out panic. If you feel comfortable, then you really haven't left your Comfort Zone, and you're not likely to make much progress. If you feel panic, then you may have gone farther than you're ready to go just yet.

If you're uncomfortable but don't feel the need to run back to your Comfort Zone, you're where you need to be. Acknowledge the discomfort, tell yourself you're feeling it because you're in the Stretch Zone, and go ahead and stretch.

It doesn't matter how small your step into the Stretch Zone looks to others. What matters is how it feels to you. If it feels like a stretch – if it feels uncomfortable but manageable – then it's the right step for you.

Take that step or similar steps enough times that they begin to feel comfortable. When they do, take some time to celebrate. You've expanded your Comfort Zone, moved your Stretch Zone nearer to your goal, and gotten closer to achieving what used to feel impossible.

Now what?

You guessed it. Take a step out of your newly expanded Comfort Zone and keep pushing closer to your goal.

You probably never thought you'd get this far. Now it's time to go even farther.

The Confidence of Character

As you push your Stretch Zone closer to your goal, you're likely to find yourself developing a greater sense of self-confidence, not just from mastering new skills, but also from summoning the courage to consistently push yourself beyond your Comfort Zone.

I think of these two kinds of confidence as the Confidence of Competence and the Confidence of Character.

The Confidence of Competence is what we usually think of when we think about confidence; it's the confidence we gain from being good at things. But the Confidence of Character is even more powerful.

The Confidence of Character comes from having the courage to do things we aren't good at yet, and to stick with them even when doing so is hard and uncomfortable.

Just as we form opinions about others by seeing what they do and drawing conclusions from it, we form opinions about ourselves by observing what *we* do. And when we see ourselves exhibiting the strength of character necessary to risk leaving our Comfort Zones again and again in pursuit of goals that matter to us, we rightly conclude that we're courageous and persistent people, that those admirable traits are essential parts of who we are, and that we'll be able to use them again and again in the pursuit of other important goals.

Once we gain the Confidence of Character, we can summon it whenever we need it, because it doesn't depend on our already being good at something before it gives us the courage to try.

That's why I say the Confidence of Competence can take us far, but the Confidence of Character can take us anywhere.

CONCLUSION
AN ENDING AND A BEGINNING

Often when you think you're at the end of something, you're at the beginning of something else.

Fred Rogers

What's Next?

We've come to the end of our *Short Course in Happiness*. Thank you for joining me on this journey.

As Mr. Rogers, the philosopher of my youth, points out, what feels like the end of something is often the beginning of something else. So I hope the end of this book leaves you inspired to make the next chapter of your life the best one yet.

I'd be happy to answer any questions you might have about this material, or to hear about how you choose to use it. And if you're interested in going further in applying these insights and techniques in your life, I'd be delighted to speak with you about my coaching services and workshops, which I offer both in-person and over the phone and internet.

Whether you're coping with changes in your life or work, looking for support in achieving personal or professional goals, or simply interested in deepening the skills and understanding you can use to create greater happiness in your life, I'd love to have the chance to speak with you about how we might work together to help you get to where you want to go.

I hope you'll get in touch by visiting my website at lyndawallace.com or emailing me at lyndawallace@me.com.

I wish you the very best on your journey.

- *Lynda*

ACKNOWLEDGEMENTS

My Gratitude List

As we saw in Chapter Two, listing five of the people, experiences, or things we're grateful for every night before bed can help us get into the habit of looking for reasons to be happy throughout the day, which can have a powerful effect on our emotional well-being.

So even though it's the middle of the afternoon on a Friday, here are five of the many people I'm grateful to for their contributions to this book.

My delightful daughter Evie, for her smart, honest reactions and suggestions, and for giving me the chance to be such a happy mom.

My wonderful parents, for their steadfast love and encouragement, and for teaching me so many of life's most important lessons.

The Positive Psychology researchers whose work I describe in this book, for the intelligence and heart they bring to such an important field.

Dr. Tal Ben-Shahar, Dr. Robert Biswas-Diener, and my other extraordinary teachers, for helping me to prepare for and thrive in this career that I love. (Interested readers will find some of Dr. Ben-Shahar's and Dr. Biswas-Diener's books listed in Sources.)

The very generous readers of activehappiness.com, for their interest and feedback as I developed the themes that I eventually incorporated into this book.

SOURCES

Introduction: The Four Elements of Happiness

Happier: Learn the Secrets to Daily Joy and Lasting Fulfillment, by Tal Ben-Shahar, Ph.D., McGraw Hill, 2007

Authentic Happiness: Using the New Positive Psychology to Realize Your Potential for Lasting Fulfillment, Martin Seligman, Simon & Schuster, 2002

The How of Happiness: A New Approach to Getting the Life You Want, by Sonja Lyubomirsky, Penguin, 2008

The Courage Quotient: How Science Can Make You Braver, by Robert Biswas-Diener, Jossey-Bass, 2012

Section One: Cultivate the Positive

The Emotional Life of Your Brain: How Its Unique Patterns Affect the Way You Think, Feel, and Live—and How You Can Change Them, by Richard J. Davidson and Sharon Begley, Hudson St. Press, March 2012

The Happiness Hypothesis: Finding Modern Truth in Ancient Wisdom, by Jonathan Haidt, Basic Books 2005

Chapter 1: Optimism

Authentic Happiness: Using the New Positive Psychology to Realize Your Potential for Lasting Fulfillment, Martin Seligman, Simon & Schuster, 2002

Stumbling on Happiness, by Daniel Gilbert, Random House, 2006

Happiness: Unlocking the Secrets of Psychological Wealth, by Ed Diener and Robert Biswas-Diener, Wiley-Blackwell, 2008

Chapter 2: Gratitude

Aging with Grace: What the Nun Study Teaches Us About Leading Longer, Healthier, and More Meaningful Lives, by David Snowdon, Bantam, 2008

Being Happy: You Don't Have to Be Perfect to Lead a Richer, Happier Life, by Tal Ben-Shahar, McGraw Hill, 2009

Chapter 4: Kindness

Pay It Forward, by Elizabeth Svoboda, Psychology Today, October, 2010

The Path to Purpose: How Young People Find Their Calling in Life, by William Damon, Simon and Schuster, 2008

Certificate in Positive Psychology Lectures, by Tal Ben-Shahar, Kripalu Institute, 2012

Chapter 5: Exercise

The Association Between Exercise Participation and Well-Being, A Co-Twin Study, by J.H. Stubbe and colleagues, Preventative Medicine, February 2007

Depression and Anxiety: Exercise Eases Symptoms, by the Staff of the Mayo Clinic, mayoclinic.com

People Who Exercise on Work Days are Happier, Suffer Less Stress, and are More Productive, Daily Mail Online, dailymail.co.uk/news/article-1095783

Chapter 6: Gaining Perspective

The Happiness Hypothesis: Finding Modern Truth in Ancient Wisdom, by Jonathan Haidt, Basic Books 2005

Effects of Self-Focused Rumination on Negative Thinking and Interpersonal Problem Solving, by Sonja Lyubomirsky and Susan Nolen-Hoeksema, Journal of Personality and Social Psychology, 1995

Manage Your Energy, Not Your Time, by Tony Schwartz and Catherine McCarthy, Harvard Business Review, October, 2007

Construal-Level Theory of Psychological Distance, by Yaacov Trope and Nira Libeman, National Institutes of Health Public Access Author Manuscript, August 2011

Chapter 7: Talking Back to Anxiety

Principles of Cognitive Behavioural Treatment, by John R. Cook, Aegis Psychological Services Inc., 1988

Certificate in Positive Psychology Lectures, by Tal Ben-Shahar, Kripalu Institute, 2012

Chapter 8: Solving Problems

Practicing Positive Psychology Coaching: Assessment, Activities, and Strategies for Success, by Robert Biswas-Diener, John Wiley and Sons, 2010

Chapter 9: Practicing Self-Compassion

Self-Compassion: Stop Beating Yourself Up and Leave Insecurity Behind, by Kristen Neff, William Morrow, 2011

Promoting Self-Compassionate Attitudes Toward Eating Among Restrictive and Guilty Eaters, by Claire E. Adams and Mark R. Leary, Journal of Social and Clinical Psychology, 2007

The Pursuit of Perfect: How to Stop Chasing Perfection and Start Living a Richer, Happier Life, by Tal Ben-Shahar, McGraw-Hill, 2009

Section Three: Developing Strong Relationships

Very Happy People, by Ed Diener and Martin E.P. Seligman, Psychological Science, January 2002

Why Are Some People Happier Than Others? The Role of Cognitive and Motivational Processes in Well-Being, by Sonja Lyubomirsky, American Psychologist, March 2001

Cross-Cultural Evidence for the Fundamental Features of Extraversion, by Richard E. Lucas and Ed Diener, Journal of Personality and Social Psychology, 2000

Positively Happy: Routes to Sustainable Happiness, by Sonja Lyubomirsky and Jaime Kurtz, Positive Acorn, 2008

Chapter 10: What the Happiest Couples Do

Why Marriages Succeed or Fail, and How You Can Make Yours Last, by John Gottman, Simon & Schuster, 1995

10 Lessons to Transform Your Marriage, John Gottman, Three Rivers Press, 2006

Chapter 11: The Surprising Truth About Extroversion

An Intraindividual Process Approach to the Relationship Between Extraversion and Positive Affect: Is Acting Extraverted as "Good" as Being Extraverted? by William Fleeson, Adrianne Malanos, and Noelle Achille, Journal of Personality and Social Psychology, 2002

Cross-Cultural Evidence for the Fundamental Features of Extraversion, by Richard E. Lucas and Ed Diener, Journal of Personality and Social Psychology, 2000

Advanced Positive Interventions Lectures, by Robert Biswas-Diener, Positive Acorn, 2012

Chapter 13: The Power of Forgiveness

The How of Happiness: A New Approach to Getting the Life You Want, by Sonja Lyubomirsky, Penguin, 2008

Learning to Forgive May Improve Well-Being, Mayo Clinic, Science Daily, January 4, 2008

Chapter 14: Setting Goals

The Happiness Hypothesis: Finding Modern Truth in Ancient Wisdom, by Jonathan Haidt, Basic Books 2005

Happier: Learn the Secrets to Daily Joy and Lasting Fulfillment, by Tal Ben-Shahar, McGraw-Hill, 2007

How to Achieve Anything, by Jeremy Dean, PsyBlog, www.spring.org.uk

Chapter 16: Staying on Track

Construal-Level Theory of Psychological Distance, by Yaacov Trope and Nira Libeman, National Institutes of Health Public Access Author Manuscript, August, 2011

Procrastination and Self-Regulatory Failure: An Introduction to the Special Issue, Journal of Rational-Emotive and Cognitive-Behavior Therapy, by T. A. Pychl and G. L. Flett, March 2012

Chapter 17: Achieving Your Most Challenging Goals

Certificate in Positive Psychology Lectures, by Tal Ben-Shahar, Kripalu Institute, 2012

Made in the USA
Charleston, SC
18 September 2015